YOUR HEART IS

CALLING

Raise a Heart-Centered Child:

Activities to Inspire Family Conversations About Our Interconnectedness

Balboa Press books may be ordered through booksellers or by contacting:

Balboa Press
A Division of Hay House
1663 Liberty Drive
Bloomington, IN 47403
www.balboapress.com
844-682-1282

Because of the dynamic nature of the Internet, any web addresses or links contained in this book may have changed since publication and may no longer be valid. The views expressed in this work are solely those of the author and do not necessarily reflect the views of the publisher, and the publisher hereby disclaims any responsibility for them.

Any people depicted in stock imagery provided by Getty Images are models, and such images are being used for illustrative purposes only.
Certain stock imagery © Getty Images.

ISBN: 978-1-5043-9297-6 (sc)
ISBN: 978-1-5043-9298-3 (e)

Library of Congress Control Number: 2017918077

Print information available on the last page.

Balboa Press rev. date: 06/16/2023

BALBOA.PRESS
A DIVISION OF HAY HOUSE

Dedication

This book is dedicated to my wonderful and loving grandchildren. They enjoyed participating in the development of the activities. Their approach to the learning was naturally inquisitive, and their excitement was inspiring. I know that they represent all children in their enthusiasm and wide-eyed wonder as they learned about the interconnectedness of all things.

Introduction

Love is all around us. As we take a moment to reflect, we will be enriched and we will find a closer bond with our child as we share and guide and listen to their observations and their inquiries. Adults play an important part as they respond to the child's questions and interests. This enhances their relationship through conversation and communication. As they gain in this awareness and communication, children are better able to transform discouragement, lack of direction, and lack of focus, into a feeling of resilience. It is important to activate this key capability in children that is a critical component of a heart centered life: *Awareness*. Awareness of self. Awareness of others. Awareness of nature and the world around them.

This manifests as more confidence, a sense of service through positive action and carrying a stronger internal compass, so they can maintain their focus and stay securely on a path of awareness and heart centered action for the rest of their lives

Over the span of several years, this series of children's books came forth in a variety of ways and moments as the concept of interconnectedness tumbled onto the page and brought the feeling of spiritual love and support to the youngest of readers through these selections. I have enjoyed writing this series of children's literature. In reading them to our younger family members, it became evident that their perspective was changing and that they were looking at nature and the world differently.

I decided to develop this book of activities that could be used in conjunction with the children's book series. In this way, parents and caregivers and the children could reflect on the concepts and develop heart centered action through conversations that were inspired by doing the activities together.

Parents are the first responders when the children are curious about the world or about spirituality. It is hoped that parents will enjoy these activities and the opportunity they afford for conversation around these topics. Grandparents can also be available to the children. Dr. Lisa Miller has written that:

> *Very often a grandparent becomes this special spiritual partner even when the parents are healthy and functional and spiritually supportive. In our busy lives, so often it is a grandparent who sits and listens to a child's questions, welcomes a child's feelings, and has the long deep talks at the kitchen table… and how spiritual parenting is an unparalleled source of resilience for children. (Lisa Miller, Ph.D. 80)*

In addition, the words of Joan Chittister, OSB, resonate and share an additional insight about how much nature plays a part in our perception of God and the need to notice and be one with our surroundings. I have been blessed by Joan Chittister's words:

> *I have come to understand that the voice of God is all around me. God is not a silent God. God is speaking to me all the time. In everything. Through everyone. I am only now beginning to listen, let alone to hear. In bare trees, I hear God saying that it is possible to die over and over again and yet survive. In the stones of this Irish landscape, I hear God saying that there is nothing that can't be endured. Not the storm, not the wind, not even the passage of time. (Joan Chittister, OSB, 185)*

Consequently, these activities are available to anyone who wishes to inspire a conversation about interconnectedness. You may be a parent or a grandparent, a caregiver or a camp counselor.

You… are the one we've been waiting for…

- Marian S. Taylor

 # Using This Activity Book

This book is intended to be used with the following children's literature selections by author Marian S. Taylor:

Where There Is Love, We Are One
Coming Down, Looking Up
See Only Love
I AM With You All Ways
We Are the Trees
Messages in the Clouds
Angels Amongst Us

The lessons are designed to provide experiences through a variety of modalities. Most of the activities are hands-on experiences, and adult supervision is recommended with younger children.

As you read through the lessons, you will see that Howard Gardner's Theory of Multiple Intelligences has been incorporated. The vocabulary from this theoretical base is used to categorize the activities within the lessons:

- Linguistic Intelligence
- Logical Intelligence
- Kinesthetic Intelligence
- Spatial Intelligence
- Musical Intelligence
- Interpersonal Intelligence
- Intrapersonal Intelligence

These books and activities can be used at home, in a camp setting, in a group setting or anywhere children explore their worlds. The intent is to have children interact with the natural world.

The activities are presented to encourage them to observe nature and the people and circumstances around them. It is hoped that children will start to observe their surroundings, to experience the world from a little different perspective, and to gain insight into themselves..

Hopefully, all participants will interact with the natural world through engaging in these activities. In this way, and through the conversations with the adults who are working with them, the participants will be introduced to the concept of awareness. It is the conversations that are paramount. The activities may not be new, but your interaction with the child is the key to understanding. As they experience their surroundings, it is your opportunity to share your heart and your inner-most thoughts. This is an opportunity to share your faith and to encourage the child in the concepts that are important to you.

These activities can be done at home or in group settings. I have referred to the caregiver as parent or grandparent, but this can also be a camp counselor. I have referred to the participant as the child or children, but in a camp or church setting, these can be students. Please know that the identifiers do not matter. What matters is the interactions and conversations that take place allowing the child to gain in awareness and a stronger internal compass.

As you look through the activities, you will see several speech bubbles with the word *Conversation* written in them. These are examples of conversations that you could have with the children. The conversations are in no way intended to be limited to these suggestions, rather the examples are merely that… examples of the kind of conversation that assists the child in noticing the world around them and recognizing the miracle that Life is…

Albert Einstein tells us, "*There are only two ways to live your life: as though nothing is a miracle, or as though everything is a miracle.*"

It is my hope that the conversations, that are inspired by the activities in this book and the reading of the other books in the series, will bring us all to the place where we see miracles everywhere in everything.

Where There Is Love...
We Are One

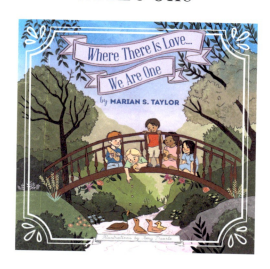

Goal of Lesson:

This book is written in a poetry format. The goal is to have children look at the world differently and to see Love everywhere in everything. It is hoped that our differences recede and love becomes the unifying factor. As the children listen to the poem, it is hoped that their awareness will be heightened and that they will begin seeing Love everywhere in everyone.

Materials needed:

Where There Is Love, We Are One, by Marian S. Taylor
Writing paper
Music paper or white paper with lines drawn
Glasses or glass bottles
Small wooden spoon
Colored Paper
White Paper

1

Getting ready to read:

Ask the following questions and allow time for response:

Do you know anyone who lives in another country?

Do they speak a different language than you do?

How do you feel when you hear someone speak a different language than you do?

Reading the book:

Read: *Where There Is Love, We Are One*.

As you read, pause on each page.

Discussion questions:

Refer to *Getting ready to read* and share experiences.

Do you know anyone who lives in another country?

Have you or your child experienced any of the situations referred to in the book?

Considering the age of the child, discuss the way people are different in the book
and the ways that people are the same.

What other questions came up while you were reading the book entitled: *Where There Is Love, We Are One?*

How did you feel in discussing the questions that your child asked? Did the book help with your conversation?

Activities:

Linguistic: Language/Writing Activities

After reading *Where There Is Love, We Are One,* look at the page where everyone is at a picnic outdoors. The words on the page read as follows:

We each begin life with love in our hearts,

And each holds love for those close to them.

There is love for a parent, a sibling, a child…

There is love for relatives and friends.

If you were at this picnic, what would you be doing? Who would you be sitting or playing with?

Logic: Science and/or Math

Look at the picture closely. There are many faces inside the larger picture of the face. How many faces can you count?

Kinesthetic: Physical movement

Hugs matter!

Hugs make a difference in our lives. We feel safe when our parent or grandparent gives us a hug. We feel happy and calm when we receive a hug from someone we trust.

Could you give someone a hug today? It might be a parent or a sibling or a friend. It is important to ask them if they are okay with you hugging them.

You can also hug a stuffed animal or a pet or a tree. A welcome hug makes us feel just right.

Music

Music to my ears!

Giving children an opportunity to express themselves through music provides an avenue to expand their literacy acquisition. Encouraging students to write a line of music can strengthen their skills in writing and sentence structure.

One way to provide this opportunity can be as simple as filling several bottles with water. In this activity, children are provided with glass bottles or glasses partially filled with water. The water in each bottle is filled to a different height. On each bottle is taped a colored shape. The student taps the bottle with a small wooden spoon and records the shape (on the bottle) on a piece of music paper. You can also draw lines on a piece of white paper to represent the musical staff. As the child taps the bottle and listens to the sounds, they write them down in a line and create a line of music.

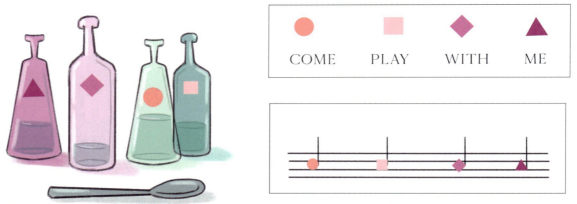

Just as a line of music needs to sound pleasing, so does a sentence. In this way we can draw comparisons between musical compositions and written compositions, thus integrating these curriculum areas. In addition, the children can write words to go with their musical compositions and again integrate music and language arts.

The feeling of joy that comes from the creation of a musical line cannot be expressed concretely, but can be seen in the faces of delighted children or heard in the words of a friend saying, "That was awesome music. Could I have a copy?" When that happens, "It's music to the ears!"

The More We Get Together by Raffi

The more we get together, together, together

The more we get together the happier we'll be.

Cause your friends are my friends

And my friends are your friends

The more we get together, the happier we'll be.

Repeat

He's Got The Whole World In His Hands by Nina Simone

He's got the whole world in his hands (4x)

He's got you and me sister in his hands (3x)

He's got the whole world in his hands.

He's got you and me brother in his hands (3x)

He's got the whole world in his hands.

He's got everybody here in his hands (3x)

He's got the whole world in his hands.

Spatial: Art

Together we're better

This project is easily done using a sheet of white copy paper.

Start at the short side of the paper and fold the paper in an accordion style. Fold about an inch and a half of the paper back upon itself. Now, fold the paper forward and then backward. Keep folding until you have folded the entire piece.

Take your scissors and carefully cut the shape of one half of a person (see the illustration). Be careful to allow the arm to go into the folded edge. Do not cut the folded edges where the arm reaches the fold. Take your scissors away and start at the bottom of the arm shape. Cut toward the body fold, but stop before you get too close. Then, turn your scissors to make the leg of the person. When you unfold the paper, you should have some interconnected stick figures.

Talk about the people in the book and the different clothing that they wear or the different skin color that was pictured. Color your stick figures to look like different people in the book. Talk about the ways they are different and the ways they are the same.

Hearts For You

We are going to make some hearts. You will need a piece of paper. It can be any color.

Fold the paper in half. On the side that has the fold, draw one half of a heart (see illustration). Please use your scissors carefully and cut along the line. When you finish cutting, unfold the paper and you will have a heart shape. You can leave it plain or you can write a note. Please give this heart to someone you care about.

KINDNESS

Kindness

Can you catch someone being kind? Can you be kind to someone else? As you go through your day, watch other people and notice when someone is being nice. If someone is kind to you, say thank you. What can you do to be a helper today? Do you have any chances to be kind to someone else?

Choose kindness. Can you think of ways to show kindness to a family member? Could you help with a younger brother or sister? Could you help with dinner or the dishes? Could you make your bed and do your homework without being asked? When you are going about your day, can you find ways to help another person? Maybe you could share a pencil or a book. Maybe you could invite another classmate to be part of an activity or a game. Maybe you could invite another classmate to sit with you or your group at lunch.

People like Mr. Rodgers dedicated their entire lives to kindness. You might enjoy reading one of his books or watching some of his television shows. He was a very kind and understanding person. It is important to be kind.

Intrapersonal or Self

Look at this picture of
the squirrel and the bunny.

Do you think they are working together
to carry the heart or do you think one is taking
it from the other? Why or why not?

How are the squirrel and the bunny the same?

How are the squirrel and the bunny different?

Even though they look different, do you
think they can be friends? Why
or why not?

Closure:

Think about all of the activities that you have done during this lesson. Name one activity that you liked the best. What was it about the activity that you most enjoyed?

Coming Down, Looking Up

Goal of Lesson:

This book is written in a poetry format. The goal is to have children look at the world differently and to see Love everywhere in everything. As the children listen to the poem, it is hoped that their awareness will be heightened.

Materials needed:

Coming Down, Looking Up, by Marian S. Taylor
Writing paper
Tempera paint or watercolors
Colored paper
Mirror, jar, flashlight
Crystal (optional)

Getting ready to read:

Ask the following questions and allow time for response.

When you ride in a car and look out the window, what do you see?

Make a list of items you might see.

If you were in the car and could only look up and out the window, what would you see?

Make a list of items you might see.

Reading the book:

Read the book, *Coming Down, Looking Up*.

As you read, pause on each page.

Discussion questions:

Refer back to *Getting ready to read* and share experiences. Children could draw pictures of things they might see as they are riding in the car.

When this child was riding in the car, what did he/she see?

This child was looking out the window and could only look up, what was he/she able to see? How did this change in perspective change what was seen?

Activities:

Linguistic: Language/Writing Activities

The following suggestions are given for creative writing activities. Reread the following selections from the book, and talk about the meaning of the words on these pages. Have the child write a sentence or two reflecting their thoughts about the phrases. They can also draw a picture to accompany their thoughts. For younger children, the parent can write the sentence for the child. The child could then draw a picture to explain the sentence.

On pages 9 and 10, the story says:

> *I can see tall poles that catch long strings and send them on their way. The lines seem endless and never stop… Where are they going today?*

What kind of strings is the story referring to? Where do you think they are going?

On pages 13 and 14, the story says:

Sometimes I see a very big truck, as it passes along my window. I wonder whatever could be inside, but I will likely never know.

What do you think could be inside the truck?

On the last page, the book refers to a story that the baby has come to tell. What would that story be about?

Logic: Science and/or Math

The following activities can be part of a discussion, or they can be done through a written response. The child may wish to include a picture.

Look at page 7.

How tall do you think the crane is?

What do the colors on the traffic light stand for?

Look at page 19 and 20.

The child sees the raindrops and then a rainbow in the sky. Have you ever seen a rainbow? How did it make you feel?

Indoor Rainbow

Younger children can make a rainbow with white paper for a cloud by gluing or taping colored strips of paper or pipe cleaners to the back of the cloud shape. See illustration.

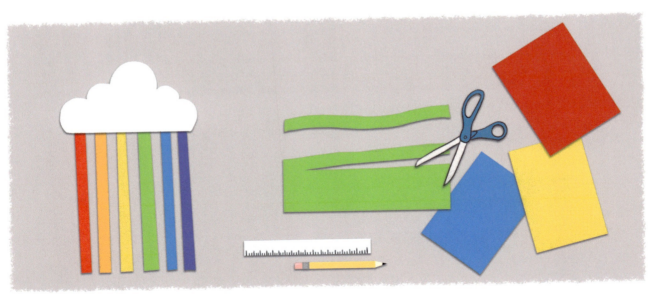

Did you know that you could make rainbows by hanging a crystal in a window and waiting for the sun to shine on the crystal? The room will be filled with rainbows. Try the following experiment to learn a little bit about how rainbows form.

Rainbow In a Jar

Everyone loves seeing a rainbow. With this activity you can now have a rainbow inside even if it hasn't been raining. Follow the simple steps on the next page and look for a rainbow.

We know the scientific explanation of how a rainbow is formed, but there is so much more. Seeing a rainbow at a special time is very meaningful. A rainbow often signifies hope. After the storm (or difficult time in our life), the sun shines through the droplets (or our tears) and the beautiful rainbow tells us that all is well.

What you need:

Circular glass jar (one quart canning jar works well) or large plain drinking glass

Flashlight

Activity

Fill the glass jar about two thirds full of water.

Take this glass jar into a very dark room with white walls.

Place the flashlight next to the jar that is filled with water. Allow the flashlight to be very close to the glass (even touching the glass) and shine the flashlight into the water. Look closely at the image on the wall. You will see the colors of the rainbow appear.

Notes:

Rainbows occur when sunlight bends as it passes through water. The sunlight bends, separating it into the colors red, orange, yellow, green, blue, indigo, and violet.

This is why you can often see a rainbow after a rain shower. The sunlight is refracted (bent) through raindrops to create a rainbow in the sky.

Kinesthetic: Physical movement

If possible, lay down on the floor of a room or on a blanket outside. Look out the window or up into the sky. What do you see?

Write down the items that you see. Younger children can draw the items on a paper.

Music:

There are many songs that bring up the thought of sunshine and rainbows. You may wish to do some research to find other songs that relate to sunshine and/or rainbows, and you can also research the full version of the songs that are listed here in an abbreviated format.

You Are My Sunshine
Composers: Jimmie Davis and Charles Mitchell (1940)

You are my sunshine

My only sunshine

You make me happy

When skies are gray

You'll never know dear

How much I love you

Please don't take my sunshine away.

Over the Rainbow
Lyricist: Yip Harburg

Somewhere over the rainbow

Way up high

Someday I'll wish upon a star

Wake up where the clouds are far behind me

Where trouble melts like lemon drops

High above the chimney tops

That's where you'll find me

Why do we think of the concept of heaven as light? There are many references to a bright light in the sky and its connection to a heavenly occurrence. If you saw a light like this, would it feel warm? Would it feel electric? Would it be bright?

Spatial Art:

On the last page of *Coming Down, Looking Up,* the child is looking at a bright light that reminds him/her of heaven. Please draw or paint a picture of a bright light in the sky. Use whatever colors you would like to express your feelings about this light that represents heaven's light shining down.

Interpersonal or Social:

Take a ride in your car with your family. Each person should name something that they see as they look out the window of the car. Talk about what you see from your car window. Do you see why the child in the book could only see things that were higher up in the sky?

The child can tell or talk about an experience they remember as a young child. The parent could share about the child or about their personal experience when they were a child.

Intrapersonal or Self:

Can you remember when you were a baby? Could you draw a picture of what you might have looked like as a baby or as a very young child?

What did you learn about each other during the conversations about the rainbow, the light, and the childhood experience?

Closure:

Think about all of the activities that you have done during this lesson. Name one activity that you liked the best. What was it about the activity that you most enjoyed?
What was most surprising about looking up and out of the window? Was there anything that you saw or experienced that surprised you or was unexpected?

 # See Only Love

Goal of Lesson:

This book is written in a poetry format. The goal is to have children look at the world differently and to see Love everywhere in everything and in everyone. As the children listen to the poem, it is hoped that their awareness will be heightened.

Materials needed:

See Only Love, by Marian S. Taylor

Copies of Sign Language and Braille Example
Blind fold
Objects such as a banana, a ball, a book
Pin Tail game
Ingredients and directions to make cupcakes
Baking soda and cornstarch
Paper and pencil
Crayons
Crutches and/or arm sling

Getting ready to read:

Ask the following questions and allow time for responses.

Ask the children if they know what it means to be blind? Discuss.

Have them close their eyes and feel an object (such as a pencil, a ball, a banana, or a book, which has been prepared ahead of time).

Can they guess what the object is?

When you can't see the object, do you notice that your sense of touch is heightened? When you can't see, do you notice sounds more or smells?

Ask the children if they know what it means to be deaf? Discuss.

Have the children cover their ears and listen for a specific sound. This sound can be the teacher's voice or a knock.

Can they guess what was said or what might have made the knocking sound?

This may be a good time to talk about how we get our eyes and ears checked on a regular basis.

When you can't hear, do you notice a smell or touch more? Are there other senses that you become more aware of?

Reading the book:

Read the book, *See Only Love*, pausing on each page.

Discussion questions:

Refer back to *Getting ready to read* and share experiences.
What did you experience when you could not see or hear?
How did this experience make you feel? Refer to the children in the book.

Activities:

Linguistic: Language/Writing Activities

Speech Generating Device: SGD
There are applications that special needs children can use that will speak for them. In the past there was a machine called a Dynavox, but more recently these children can use a special application that will speak for them. (For additional information on this type of machine, please research Dynavox.)

They can push buttons for the letters and/or words and make sentences. If you can access this application, it would be another way to show participants how special needs individuals can communicate when they do not have the capacity to speak.

Braille Template

Write your name in Braille! Look at the chart and choose the letters that are in your name.
Mark the dots in some way:
Place an X on the dots that are included in your name. (Please use the row of blank squares at the bottom of the page.)
Color the dots that are included in your name in a darker color.

When complete, an adult can punch the colored in circles with a pencil or ball point pen, from back to front. This will cause the paper to split and form a bump on the front of the paper.
Place the braille representation of the child's name, face up, so they can read it. Then, have the child close their eyes and move their fingers over the raised bumps. In this way, the student can feel/read their name in Braille.

Can you write your name in Braille in the blocks below?

How does Braille assist
a blind person in accessing the world?
How do hand signs assist a deaf person
in accessing information and communicating?
Does it help you grow in understanding of these
individuals as you learn about these methods of
communication? How would these individuals
share their beliefs?

"I love you" in
Sign Language

Sign Language

Use the pictures below to learn about Sign Language.
Learn a few basic signs.
Try to communicate at least one word in Sign Language to a friend or family member.

Here are a few signs that can be used to communicate basic needs. Try to make the signs and ask a friend to interpret what you are saying.

YES
Hand in a slight fist. Move fist up and down at the wrist.

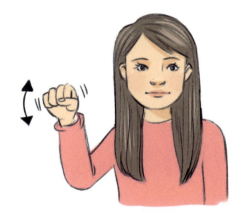

NO
Index and middle finger rest on outstretched thumb. Open and close the fingers.

GOOD

Right hand held out in front of body.
Left hand touches chin and lowers to
right hand, palms up.

THANK YOU

Hand touches chin and then lowers,
palm up.

MORE

Hold fingers out and thumb behind. Move
hands together and apart in repeated
motion.

WATER

Three fingers (index, middle and ring
finger) held straight up. Index finger
touching chin. Thumb and smallest finger
held together.

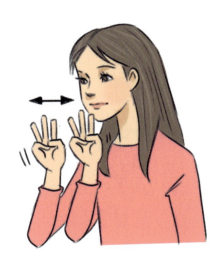

EAT
All fingers held together and touching lips.

I LOVE YOU
Thumb, index and smallest finger held upright. Middle and ring finger bent down.

COOKIE

Right hand held flat and palm up. Left hand held upright touching the palm of right hand. Left hand moves in a kind of circle back and forth.

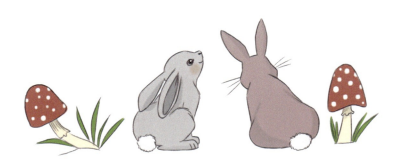

These activities are all designed to increase awareness about the differences that exist between individuals, but to also note how we are the same. The conversation can be around the idea that we all have strengths and how the saying, "together we're better" rings true. Where one is deficient another may have strength. All of our strengths and all of our weaknesses work together to make the whole. Also, as the children participate in the Kinesthetic activities, how do they feel? Does participation in these activities help in gaining understanding of the individuals with special needs?

Logic: Science and/or Math

Graphing Activity

Prepare a grid using a shower curtain, drop cloth, or large paper.
The group can decide on categories.
All participants remove one shoe and place it in one of six piles that have
been identified. Then take the shoes in the piles and place them in the column
below the category identifier. The following illustration shows the graph.

SANDALS	SNEAKERS WITH VELCRO	FLIP FLOPS	LACED SHOES	SLIP ONS	DRESS SHOES

Various math activities include:

Which categories have the most shoes?
Which categories have the least number of shoes?
Determine how many more of one kind of shoe on the graph adds up to
more than another kind of shoe on the graph.
Are there any categories that have the same number of shoes?
Include any other math equations.
How are we the same? How are we different?
Look at two different categories.
Are there parts of the shoes that are the same? For example: some
sneakers have laces and some dress shoes have laces.
Place shoes in categories according to differences.
Discuss how people can have differences (eye color, hair color, long
pants, dresses, etc.) but also have many things in common (two
arms, two feet, and even wanting to be friends.)

The goal is to have children think about the concepts in *See Only Love*. The overriding point is to have children recognize that there are differences in things as well as people, but different abilities will not change who you are as a human being. Please call attention to the differences in the shoes, while also making sure that the child realizes the ways that they are the same, ultimately getting across the point that they are all shoes.

Kinesthetic: Physical movement

Writing letters and numbers in a kinesthetic manner.

Highlighting the sense of touch which is so important in the Braille activity.

Place some play sand or Jello on a cookie sheet.

Have the students trace their name in the sand/Jello.

Have the students trace numbers in the sand/Jello.

Tasting items

Blindfold participant.
Place a paper plate in front of the student. Each plate should have food items on it.
The food items can be fruits, vegetables, or snacks.
Have the student taste the items and guess what food items are on the plate.

It is important to realize
that the senses work together. Please have a
conversation about the possibility that one sense could be
blocked; for example a person is blind. In this case, discuss how
other senses could be heightened. For example, a person who has lost
their sight may have a heightened sense of smell or hearing.
Helen Keller was a very famous person who could not hear or see. Those who
knew her observed, *"Helen is mesmerized. Nature seems wonderful, especially
after her sheltered existence. It helps her experience the entire world and all
life has to offer, despite her disabilities. Even if you are blind and deaf, you
can still enjoy nature."* Can you think of ways that you could enjoy
nature if you could not see or hear?

Obstacle Course

It is fun to set up a few activities that help the child to experience some of the challenges that a person with special needs might encounter. The activities are suggestions. You may think of other activities to include. The children can take turns as individuals, or they can work in pairs, supporting each other in a buddy system. In this way, the friend is responsible for helping the buddy as they work through the activities.

Pin the Tail on the Donkey or Smiley Face game

Place a drawing of a donkey or a smiley face on the wall or door.

Give student a drawing of a tail (for the donkey) or a nose (for the face).

Blindfold the child.

Direct child to move toward the picture and put the tail on the donkey picture or the nose on the smiley face picture.

Walk with crutches

Borrow a set of crutches or a wheel chair.
Allow the child to experience using them.

Try to write or pick items up with a sling on one arm

Borrow a sling or make one from cloth.
Allow the students to experience what it is like to have a sling and how it restricts their movement.

After using the crutches or the wheel chair or a sling, discuss how each item affected your ability to move and perform basic tasks. How did this make you feel? Were there things that you could not do? If you were not able to participate in your usual way, did you feel separated from the group or alone?

Music:

Here are two songs that lend themselves to this theme.
You may wish to research other selections that would express love and understanding of all individuals. In addition, you can also have the participants put their own words together and sing them to a familiar tune.

We Are the World
By Michael Jackson and Lionel Ritchie (1985)

We are the world, we are the children

We are the ones who make a brighter day

So let's start giving

There's a choice we're making

We're saving our own lives

It's true we'll make a better day

Just you and me.

Jesus Loves the Little Children
By C.H.Woolston and G. F. Root (1976)

Jesus loves the little children

All the children of the world

All are children in the Light

All are precious in his sight

Jesus loves the little children of the world.

Helen Keller was a famous person who could not hear or see and yet she once said, *"What was my amazement to discover that I could feel, not only the vibration, but also the impassioned rhythm, the throb and the urge of the music! The intertwined and intermingling vibrations from different instruments enchanted me."* What senses do you think Helen was using? Can you give examples?

Spatial: Art

Fingerpaint and exploring touch

It is best to purchase finger paint paper. It has a heavier consistency.

Place measured amounts of colored finger paint on paper plates.

The students can take a small amount of paint onto their paper and make designs with the paint.

Punched Tin Foil Art

Many of the projects are representative of several of the intelligences. This project includes measuring and deciphering fractions. It is also very spatial.

Baking Soda Clay Recipe
Courtesy of Mudworks, by MaryAnn F. Kohl, who calls it Play Clay.

Mix 1 cup baking soda and 1/2 cup cornstarch in a saucepan
Add 2/3 cup warm water and stir until smooth
Over medium heat, boil and stir until it is the consistency of mashed potatoes
Put on a board to cool some, knead it and play away!
Store leftover clay in an airtight container. This will keep for several weeks
Modeled figures will air dry very quickly and are pure white in color

Make the recipe. It does not take a great amount of time, but should be stirred consistently when it is on the stove. Once it is ready, it can be placed on a piece of card stock paper. Flatten out the clay and then cover with tin foil that is thicker than normal and quite sturdy.

The student can then use a popsicle stick or finger to push into the foil and make a design. In the sample, a wheelchair design was made in the foil. Other special needs designs are included under the Spatial category.

The student could also do their name in Braille. The clay has many design possibilities. A frame was placed on the design in the sample. This recipe makes about one cup of clay.

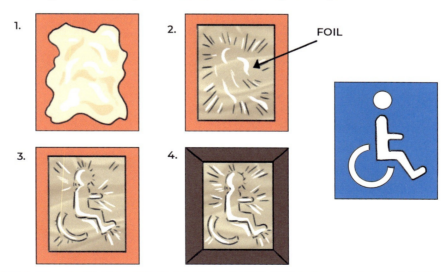

Cupcakes

Cooking is a way to have fun and express creativity. It can also incorporate math skills as well as creative expression. These cupcakes can be decorated with eye glasses (gives understanding that glasses are also an accommodation) and/or Special Needs Symbols. These symbols help to indicate accommodations for individuals with special needs.

Why do you think that
the symbols below were chosen
to represent the special need that is
characterized by the picture?

Interpersonal: Social

In many communities, there are events in which special needs children can participate. If it is difficult to find actual events, pictures or videos of children participating in these activities might be found through researching the topics.

If possible, participants could take a field trip to visit one or more of these activities in their community:
    Ice Skating
    Sailing
    Swimming
    Horseback Riding
    Cheerleading

Intrapersonal: Self

Refer back to the activities in the section called *Getting ready to read*.

How did you feel when you could not see?

How did you feel when you could not hear?

Write or dictate a sentence. Participants can express their thoughts through words or pictures.

Closure:

How did you feel when you could not hear?

How did you feel when you could not see?

How did you feel when you could not walk or you could not pick items up when you were wearing a sling?

It is important to recognize that everyone has needs or things they cannot do as well as someone else, but we are all special in our own way and have love to share.

You have had many conversations during this chapter. What did you learn about your child during your conversations? As the caregiver, what insight did you gain?

I Am With You All Ways

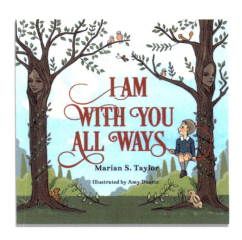

Goal of Lesson:

This book is written in a poetry format. The goal is to have children look at the world differently and to see Love everywhere in everything. As the children listen to the poem, it is hoped that their awareness will be heightened, and that they will begin seeing Love everywhere in everything.

Materials needed:

I AM With You All Ways, by Marian S. Taylor
Heart rocks
Pictures of clouds, trees, and rainbows
Tempera paint
Paper (tissue paper or printer paper in legal size)
Apples (cut them in half around the middle)
Paper for writing exercises
Camera (optional)

Getting ready to read:

Ask the following questions and allow time for response.

Have you ever seen a cloud that looked like a shape?
Take responses and allow them to describe.

Have you ever seen a rainbow?
Take responses and allow them to describe how it felt to see the rainbow colors.

Reading the book:

Read *I AM With You All Ways*, pausing on each page. Have the child look at the photographs and then at the illustrations. What are the similarities? What are the differences between the illustrations and the photographs?

As you look at the illustrations, discuss how an actual photograph differs from an illustration.

Activities:

Linguistic: Language/Writing Activities

The following suggestions are given for creative writing activities.
Reread the following selections from the book and talk about the meaning of the words on these pages.
Have the child write a sentence or two reflecting their thoughts about the phrases. They can also draw
  a picture to accompany their thoughts. For younger children, the leader can write the sentence for
  the child. The child could then draw a picture to explain the sentence. Each of these selections
  inspires a specific conversation. Enjoy this opportunity to learn more.

Look at pages 8 and 9. This cloud looks like a dove flying by. Where do you think this dove is going?

Look at pages 12 and 13. If you saw this angel in the sky, what would she be saying to you?

Look at pages 14 and 15. These animals are hiding in the roots of this tree. What would they be saying to each other? Why would they be hiding?

Look at pages 16 and 17. This tree has a face in the side of the trunk. If you saw this tree, what would you say to the tree?

Logic: Science and/or Math

Talk about and look at representations of shapes: Circle, square, triangle, rectangle, and heart shape.

Go out of doors and look for shapes in nature. For example: a flower or a tree nut might have a circular shape. A pine tree might have a triangular shape. Rocks and stones can have many shapes like a circle, square, triangle, rectangle, or heart shape. Please look for heart shapes.

If you are unable to go out of doors, you might find some photos of natural objects that you could use to show shapes in nature and make the same point.

Kinesthetic: Physical movement

Go outdoors and take some pictures with a camera or cell phone. Each child should take one picture and then try to draw or paint that picture. These could be displayed with the photograph taped or stapled to the drawing.

Music:

There are many songs to express love. You may wish to research other selections that would express love and the feeling of unity. In addition, you can have the children put their own words to the tune of a familiar melody. Here is one to enjoy.

From a Distance
By Julie Gold (1985)

From a distance there is harmony

And it echoes through the land

And it's the hope of hopes, it's the love of loves

It's the heart of every man

It's the hope of hopes, it's the love of loves

This is the song of every man

And God is watching us, God is watching us

God is watching us from a distance

That's the Glory of Love
By Billy Hill (1936)

You've got to give a little, take a little,

and let your poor heart break a little.

That's the story of, that's the glory of love.

You've got to laugh a little, cry a little,

until the clouds roll by a little.

That's the story of, that's the glory of love.

Spatial: Art

Star Magic

Take an apple round and red.
Don't slice down.
Slice through instead.
Right inside it you will see
A star as pretty as can be.

Margaret Hillert

Wrapping paper activity (or a piece of construction paper for apple prints)

Give each child a large sheet of tissue paper or newsprint.
Place different colors of tempera paint on individual paper plates.

Cut several apples in half. The cut is through the fleshy part of the apple, not stem to stem. When you cut the apple in half this way, you will see that the seed area at the center of the apple will look like a star inside the apple. The apple is then dipped into the paint and the print is stamped onto the paper in a repeated manner. The child can experiment with the amount of paint. Too much paint will not allow the star to show when the apple is stamped onto the paper.

Making the prints on a piece of construction paper.

    The child can dictate a sentence or they can write a sentence about the star inside of them.
The star inside of them is the special part of them, something they like to do or something they
are really good at or something that they feel is special about them.

They could respond to the prompt: I AM...
It is important to focus on things like being nice to others, helping family or
friends, or something that is a special gift they possess. For example: I AM Love, I AM kind to
others. I AM an artist. I AM a musician.

Each of us has a gift or
dream to share with others. We have
the gift of creativity, the gift of kindness,
the gift of discovery, the gift of sport, the gift of
understanding, the gift of helping, etc. Think about
the star inside the apple as the star inside of *you*, or
your heart's desire, or your gift, your dream. What do
you dream about doing or being? What is your gift
to life? Enjoy a conversation about hopes and
dreams.

Interpersonal: Social

Have the children sit in a circle and share their ideas about expressing the star inside of them. What is it that they see inside of themselves. It would be wonderful if they could talk about the gifts of their classmates and share with each other. What is the star inside their friends?

Intrapersonal: Self

Give each child a mirror or have them share a mirror. Allow the children to look into the mirror and then draw a picture of themselves. When they look in the mirror or at the picture, they could repeat: *I love you. I really love you.* It is important to love yourself and practice self-care. It allows for a healthy outlook and soul discovery.

Discussion questions:

Refer back to *Getting ready to read* and share experiences.
Let the participants handle some heart rocks or look at the picture on pages 6 and 7.

> The idea is to look at nature differently, to see shapes and visuals in nature and in all creation, that clearly give us the idea that Spirit is everywhere in everything.

Closure

Take the participants outdoors and look for rocks that are shaped like a heart.

If there are clouds in the sky, look for shapes in the clouds and have fun talking about them and guessing what they might represent or what shape they look like.

What did you learn about your child during your conversations? As the caregiver, what did you learn about yourself?

We Are The Trees

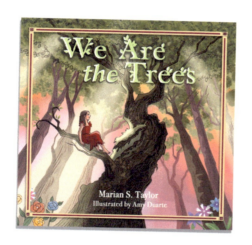

Goal of Lesson:

This book is written in a poetry format. The goal is to have children look at the world differently and to see Love everywhere in everything. As the children listen to the poem, it is hoped that their awareness will be heightened.

Materials needed:

We Are the Trees, by Marian S. Taylor
Pictures of trees
Leaves to observe
Paper
Paints (green and brown)
Make Your Own Paper materials
Writing paper for activities
The Giving Tree, by Shel Silverstein

Getting ready to read:

Ask the following questions and allow time for response:
Show pictures of different trees. Ask the children if they have any trees in their yard at home?

Look out the window of the room and notice any trees.

If possible, have several leaves for the children to look at and talk about the different shapes.

How do trees help us in our world? What do they do for us? Try to elicit responses such as, give us shade, give us wood to make fires to keep us warm, and have fruit on them like apples or oranges. Some children may know that they clean our air by taking in carbon dioxide and releasing oxygen.

Reading the book:

Read the book, *We Are the Trees*, pausing on each page. Talk about the different trees and the shapes and how they make the child feel.

Discussion questions:

Refer back to *Getting ready to read* and share experiences.
Did you have a favorite picture in the book? Why did you like it?
Have you ever sat under a tree on a hot day? How did you feel?

Activities:

Linguistic: Language/Writing Activities

Write a *Cinquain Poem* about trees.

This section inspires many conversations as the participant and caregiver discuss the many parts of the poem and the subject, *trees*.

Cinquain Poem

A cinquain poem is composed of five lines. It is structured as a short, but factual poem about one subject.
The lines are written in the following manner:
Line 1: Title – one word.
This is the subject matter of your cinquain poem...
For example: TREES

Line 2: Description – two words
Two things that describe your subject....
For example: TALL, GREEN

Line 3: Action – three words
Three words that say something about your title word.
These words should end with ING.
For example: SWAYING, GROWING, BLOWING

Line 4: Feeling – a phrase
A factual line about your subject.
For example: TREES COME IN MANY SHAPES AND SIZES.

Line 5: Title – one word.
This should be a synonym for your title.
For example: EVERGREEN

Poetry

Here is an excerpt from a familiar poem about a tree. You can find the full version in Joyce Kilmer's publication, *Trees and Other Poems* (1914).

Trees
By Joyce Kilmer

I think that I shall never see
A poem lovely as a tree.
A tree that looks at God all day,
And lifts her leafy arms to pray;
A tree that may in summer wear
A nest of robins in her hair;
Poems are made by fools like me,
But only God can make a tree.

Logic: Science and/or Math

Leaves

Go outdoors and find different leaves. Notice the shapes of the leaves and how they are different.

Place the leaf under some tissue paper and rub a crayon over the paper. What kind of shape do you see? Can you see the stem? Can you see the veins on the leaf?

As the children explore
their environment, they will look for a
variety of leaf shapes. As we call attention to the
different shapes and bark coverings of different trees,
we also look at the differences in the leaves. Discuss the
commonalities and differences in trees.

Circumference

Go outdoors and take a long rope with you.
Stretch the rope around a tree and mark the place where the rope meets on the tree.
Lay the rope out on the ground and measure the rope with a measuring tape or stick.
How many inches was it around the tree? This is called the circumference.

What is a main ingredient of paper? Are there different kinds of paper? Can you use old paper to make new paper? Take a moment to look up the ingredients of paper and discuss how this might impact the environment.

Make your own paper

There are many ways to make paper.

White tissue paper or newspaper, ripped into small pieces, can be placed in a blender with water.

Once the liquified tissue paper is blended, the mixture can be placed on a piece of screen or in between towels to allow the excess water to evaporate. An iron can be used on the towels.

Allow the paper to dry overnight before using it to color or write.

The newspaper mixture will be darker and thicker, while the tissue paper will turn out to be thinner and whiter.

Music:

Parts of Trees Song
By Mr. R

Roots... Trunk... Branches... Leaves
Branches... Leaves
Roots... Trunk... Branches... Leaves
Branches ... Leaves
Buds and fruits and flowers in the breeze.
Those are the parts of trees.
Repeat (the tune is *Head, shoulders, knees, and toes*)

LEAVES

BRANCHES

TRUNK

ROOTS

84

Spatial: Art

All Hands Ready for Action
There are many ways to make trees with children. The child can cut the parts of a tree from construction paper and glue these shapes onto a larger sheet of paper. The child can then color birds or fruit onto the tree. The child could also use paint and paintbrush or the child could do finger or hand painting.

To make a tree using paint, each participant should be given a sheet of large white paper. The parent or the child can draw a tree trunk on the paper with a marker or with crayons or with a paintbrush.

In choosing to use the hands or fingers to make the leaves, the paint should be evenly distributed onto paper plates for ease of access and to minimize too much mess. The child can put their hand into the paint, palm down, or they can just use a finger-tip and place it into the paint then put the paint onto the paper.

This hand or finger print can be repeated over and over until the tree leaves are completed to the artists' satisfaction.

Choice of color can depend on the season, but leaves can be green or brown or
    multicolored.
The artist can also make an evergreen tree and place colorful fingerprints
    for lights or decorations.
It is important to cover your workspace with old newspapers or a plastic
    table cover. In addition, it will be helpful to have a bucket of soapy
    water and plenty of paper towels available.

Pole of Totems

For older children, a totem pole of plaster of paris can be made. Using a tubular chip container, mix plaster of paris and fill the container. Allow to dry until still slightly soft. The chip container can be peeled off of the plaster and a popsicle stick can be used to draw a design into the plaster.

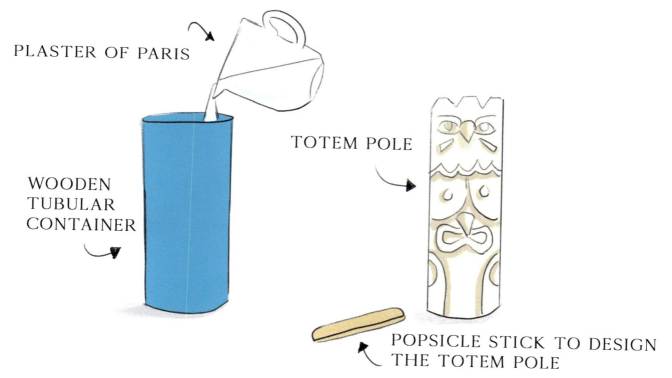

PLASTER OF PARIS

TOTEM POLE

WOODEN
TUBULAR
CONTAINER

POPSICLE STICK TO DESIGN
THE TOTEM POLE

Children can look at the totems on page 11 of *We Are the Trees*. You will notice many designs on the poles. Totems can be people, animals, birds, or objects that represent either a familiar legend or a family lineage or an event. The pole can also just be an artistic endeavor. Children can decide on three totems that represent areas of their life and etch the designs into the pole. See the sample in the picture.

Interpersonal: Social

Story Circle for *The Giving Tree*:

One child should be the boy.
One child should be the tree.
As the parent reads the story, the children sit in a circle.
As the parent reads a certain part, the tree child will repeat the part that the tree
      says, the boy will repeat what the boy says.
Then they will act out the actions that are described in the book.
The Story Circle can finish with the parent and the child talking about the
      outcomes of the story as it relates to *We Are the Trees*.

The story of *The Giving Tree* is a wonderful way to start conversation around how we look at *giving* in our lives. How does love determine our giving? Does it have an effect on how much we give? How did the boy use the gifts? Is there anything you would do differently?

Intrapersonal: Self

Pretend you are sitting on a leaf that is way up high in the top of a tree.

The leaf lets go from the tree and begins to fall to the ground.
You are riding the leaf from the top of the tree down to the ground.
Can you describe what you might see as you pass by the branches of the
    tree and make your way to the ground? Do you see any animals or birds? Do you
    see any insects?
Where does the leaf land?

Describe how you
feel as you float down to the
ground, riding on the leaf.

Hug a Tree

Go outdoors, place your arms around a tree and hug the tree.
Do you feel anything? What do you feel?
Ask the tree a question. What thoughts come to your mind?

Hugging a tree brings
a variety of feelings; just spend
the time and receive.

Closure:

Refer back to *Getting ready to read* questions.
What have we learned about trees? Did you learn something that you did not know before?

 # Messages In The Clouds

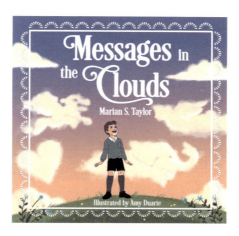

Goal of Lesson:

This book is written in a poetry format. The goal is to have children look at the world differently and to see Love everywhere in everything. As the children listen to the poem, it is hoped that their awareness will be heightened.

Materials needed:

Messages in the Clouds, by Marian S. Taylor
Blue construction paper
White paint
Cotton balls
Pillows
String, rope, or rolled towel
Balloons
Glass jar with lid

Getting ready to read:

Bring the children together on a story rug or in a story circle. The parent should have some pictures of clouds to show the children. As the parent shows the pictures, the following questions can be pondered: allow time for response.

> Show some pictures of clouds. The parent can use a page out of the book,
>   for example, the picture of the elephant cloud or another picture.
> Does this picture look like any kind of shape, animal, object? Allow time
>   for response.
> Have you ever seen a cloud that looks like a picture of something? Allow
>   time for response.
> What did it look like? Allow children to say something that they have seen.

Note: You can also use the book, *It Looked Like Spilt Milk*, by Charles Shaw to provide examples of shapes in the clouds. This book could give the children an opportunity to look at shapes and see the abstract concepts. After this preparation, they will be read the *Messages in the Clouds* book which has actual pictures of clouds.

Reading the book:

Read the book, *Messages in the Clouds*, pausing on each page. Ask the children if they see the shape referred to in the poem.

Discussion questions:

Refer back to *Getting ready to read* and share experiences.
What shapes do you remember from the pictures in the book?
What was your favorite picture?
Why was it your favorite picture?

Activities:

Linguistic: Language/Writing Activities

There are several art activities listed in this section. After the children create the pictures, engage them in a discussion about their picture. Depending on the age of the participant, the child can write a sentence that describes the picture or the parent can write a sentence dictated by a younger child.

Depending on the age of the children, they could write a story about the picture. They could include what they think the cloud design looks like or what it might mean to them.

Logic: Science and/or Math

Making a Cloud

Can you see a cloud inside your house? Where would it be? How do clouds form?
What are they made of? Use a jar, some ice, and water to make a cloud.
Some call this kitchen science. There are many experiments that you can do right
in your own home.

Materials
- a glass jar (a quart canning jar works well)
- boiled water (adult supervision needed)
- ice in a zip lock bag
- a match (adult supervision needed)

Activity

Pour some of the boiling water into the glass jar.
Swish it around to warm the sides of the jar.
Place a sandwich size plastic bag containing ice on the top of the glass jar.
After a few moments, lift the bag of ice and quickly slip a lighted match into the
     jar. Place the bag of ice back on top of the jar.
Watch the cloud form inside the jar. When it is fully formed, remove the bag of
     ice and watch the cloud escape.

Clouds form when hot and cold (warm and cool) air masses come in contact. In this case,
     the hot water represents a hot air mass and the ice represents a cold air mass. You can
     see the cloud forming in the jar.

As you are doing this
experiment, you can be talking
with the child about how the warm and
cool components of air are coming together. You
might also bring attention to the way that nature is
responsible for the cloud forming, but how special it
is that these clouds sometimes take on very special
shapes. An animal shape or an angel wing can
bring a special feeling. Talk about how it feels
to see these special shapes.

Kinesthetic: Physical movement

Obstacle course (inside or outside)

Have the child pretend they are an airplane and fly amongst the clouds. Put out pillows or paper markers that they need to touch in their flight.

Blow up some balloons. Hang them from underneath a table. Children can try to go through the balloons without making them move.

Stretch a string on the floor. Place a pillow at either end of the string. Children can try to walk along the string as if they are balancing in the sky.

The obstacle course is intended to help with environmental awareness, being aware of what is around you and noticing the nuances of our surroundings.

Music:

After reading the book, *Messages in the Clouds*, the students can sing the following song: *Both Sides, Now* is a popular song which was most memorably written by Joni Mitchell. The lines that tell us about clouds are very appropriate for this book.

Both Sides, Now
By Joni Mitchell

Bows and flows of angel hair and ice cream castles in the air

And feather canyons everywhere, I've looked at clouds that way

But now they only block the sun they rain and snow on everyone

So many things I would have done, but clouds got in my way

I've looked at clouds from both sides now

From up and down and still somehow

It's cloud's illusions I recall

I really don't know clouds at all

Spatial Art:

Paint Blob Clouds

Each child should have a piece of blue paper and a small blob of white paint. Depending on the age of the child, the blob of white paint should be placed in the center of the blue paper.

The parent can assist younger children as the blue paper is folded in half with the paint inside.

Once the fold has been appropriately creased, the paper should be opened and allowed to dry.

The child should be encouraged to write about what they think the shape of the white paint looks like on the page. What shape or object does the child see in the shape of the white paint? Does the shape have meaning?

Air Streams

Each child should have a piece of blue paper and some white paint that
    has been thinned.

Depending on the age of the child, the white paint should be placed in the
    center of the blue paper.

The parent can assist younger children in taking a straw and blowing the
    paint in different directions on the paper. This will make an
    interesting shape. Allow the paint to dry.

The child should be encouraged to write about what they think it looks
    like. What shape or object do you see in the shape of the white paint
    on the blue paper? Does the shape of the white paint have meaning?

Poofs of Cotton

Each child should have a piece of blue paper and several white cotton balls.

The child will glue the cotton balls on the paper to make a design that looks like a cloud.

The child should be encouraged to write about what they think it looks like. What shape or object do you see in the shape of the cotton balls on the blue paper? Does the shape of the cotton have meaning?

As you and your child work on these art projects, there is an opportunity to reflect on your experiences with clouds and cloud formations. Have fun talking about clouds and using your imaginations. Be inspired!

Rainbow cloud

You may wish to have younger children make a rainbow cloud instead of working with the boiling water in the previous activity. The child should cut a cloud shape from white paper (they can glue cotton on this shape if they wish). They can then glue pieces of colored paper or pipe cleaners to the back of the white cloud. The colored objects should be in the ROYGBIV sequence of the colors of the rainbow.

Interpersonal: Social

The children can work together during the science experiment. As they follow the steps for making a cloud, they will need to cooperate and collaborate.

After the children make their cloud pictures, they can share their pictures and stories. This is most effective in a story circle.

Intrapersonal: Self

Depending on the climate and the availability of a grassy area, the children should be encouraged to lay or sit on a towel and watch the clouds in the sky. The children should be given time to look at the clouds and identify any shapes they might see.

It is so important to teach children, as well as adults, to just be… It is important to just breathe… The hope is that you and your child will take some time to lie down and just be with nature. How does it feel to be outdoors in the fresh air and breathe in deeply? What do you observe? Is there a breeze? Do you hear any nature sounds? Do you see any clouds? Do you see any shapes in the clouds? How do you feel about the shapes you see? How do you feel about this experience? Has this experience inspired a conversation with your child or with another adult?

Closure:

The children should be encouraged to discuss their experiences with the book and the activities in these lessons. It is important to be accepting of all responses and to allow children to reflect and look at the world differently and to make connections with the natural world.

> What did we learn from our experiment about how clouds are formed?
> What cloud shapes were in the book and in your art work?
> What did you like about your art work and the shape of your cloud?
> Will you continue to look for shapes in the clouds?
> Allow yourself to feel the essence of Spirit as you spend time looking at the clouds.

What did you learn
about your child or your relationship
during your conversations? As the parent
or grandparent, what insight have you gained
about your child, about yourself, and about the
interconnectedness of all things?

Angels Amongst Us

Goal of Lesson:

This book is written in a poetry format. The goal is to have children look at the world differently and to see Love everywhere in everything. As the children listen to the poem, it is hoped that their awareness will be heightened, and that they will begin seeing Spirit everywhere in everything.

Materials needed:

Angels Amongst Us, by Marian S. Taylor
Small household sponge
Tempera Paint
Paper for painting
Materials to make angel wings
     White cardboard or painted cardboard
     Novelty feathers
     Glue
     Ribbon or binding
     Square piece of cardboard
     Yarn

Getting ready to read:

Find a comfortable place to read with your child or children.
Engage the child with the following questions:

Has anyone ever done something nice for you? Can you describe what it was and
     how it made you feel?
Have you ever done a favor for someone? Can you describe how it happened? How did the other
     person respond to what you did for them?

Sometimes we do kind things that other people recognize, but sometimes we do kind things that are not
     known. Both ways of being kind are important.

Reading the book:

Read the book, *Angels Amongst Us*, pausing on each page.

Discussion questions:

Refer back to *Getting ready to read* and share experiences.
What was your favorite part of this book?
Why was it your favorite part?

Activities:

Linguistic: Language/Writing Activities

Pretend that you have your angel wings on (see Spatial: Art section).
What do you think you would do if you were an angel?
How would you help people?
What would you whisper in someone's ear to make them feel happy?

After the children have thought about these questions, engage them in a discussion. Depending on the age of the participant, the child can draw a picture and write a sentence that describes what they would do or the parent can write a sentence dictated by a younger child.

Depending on the ages of the children, they could write a story about what they would do. In either case, children could draw a picture of their angelic action and do a sponge painting to accompany their sentence or story. Refer to the Spatial: Art section to read a description of sponge painting.

There is a section in the
book where God says,

Sometimes I'm a thought in your mind that bring peace.
Sometimes I'm a familiar hug in a crowd...

I can send you a message through the words of other people.
I can send you a message through the words of a song.

What do you think these words mean? Have you ever had a thought
that was comforting? Have you ever heard a song and the words
answered a question that you had or helped to soothe your
emotions?

Logic: Science and/or Math

Stare at one of the shapes below. Look directly at the dot in the middle of the shape. Do this for at least 30 seconds then look at a white wall or a plain white piece of paper.

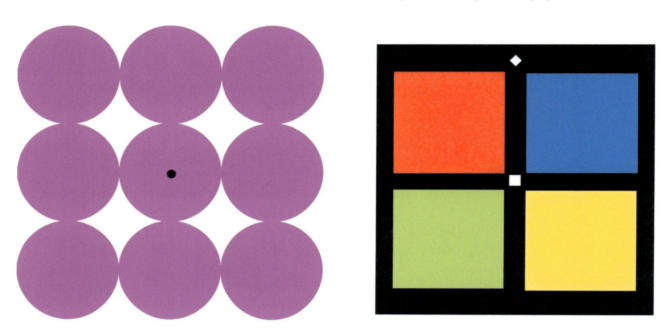

The design that you see on the white surface is called an afterimage.
What causes afterimages? Negative afterimages occur when the rods and cones, which are part of the retina, are overstimulated and become desensitized. This desensitization is strongest for cells viewing the brightest part of the image, but is weakest for those viewing the darkest.

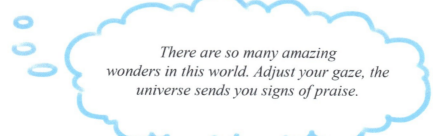

There are so many amazing wonders in this world. Adjust your gaze, the universe sends you signs of praise.

Kinesthetic: Physical movement

Angel Wings

Cut the wing shape out of a piece of cardboard.
Use white cardboard or paint the shape white or any color you wish.
Purchase novelty feathers and glue them to the cardboard. These can be glued all over the wing shapes or you can just glue on a few of the feathers.

Glue or secure a piece of ribbon or binding to the cardboard. This will tie around the child's chest or use two pieces to loop over the arms. Put on your angel wings and dance to the music in the next section.

Music:

This Little Light of Mine
By Harry Dixon Loes

This little light of mine, I'm gonna let it shine. Sing 3x
Let it shine, let it shine, let it shine.

Everywhere I go, I'm gonna let it shine. Sing 3x
Let it shine, let it shine, let it shine.

This little light of mine, I'm gonna let it shine. Sing 3x
Let it shine, let it shine, let it shine.

How did your child react to being an angel and letting his/her light shine? Talk about how we can let our light shine every day.

Music:

You Gotta Sing by Raffe

You gotta sing when the spirit says sing – 2x
When the spirit says sing
You gotta sing right along
Sing when the spirit says sing.

You gotta (insert: clap, hum, snap, swim, stomp, and hush) when the spirit says...
Finish with the verse: You gotta sing when the spirit says sing.

119

Spatial Art:

Sponge Painting

In the previous section, *Linguistic: Language/Writing Activities*, the child was asked to draw a picture to go with their story. The picture can be colored or painted to enhance the project.

You may wish to try this sponge painting activity.

Place a small amount of a few different colors of tempera paint on plates.
Cut pieces of sponge from a household sponge.
Try the sponge painting on an old newspaper first.
Have the child gently dab the sponge into the paint and then dab it onto
    their picture. They can add as much color to their picture as they wish.
The sponge makes an interesting design on the paper.

Weaving

Weaving is the interlacing of two sets of threads at right angles to each other to form cloth.
Weaving is usually done on a loom. One set of threads is called the warp. These threads are held
    taut and in parallel order on the loom by harnesses creating a space called the shed.

We are going to take a square of cardboard and draw a line one inch from the outer edge of one
    side of the cardboard square.
Next, draw a line one inch from the exact opposite side of the cardboard square.
Then, hold the ruler on the line and mark perpendicular lines one half inch apart from top to
    bottom. You will do this on both sides of the cardboard square and you will cut into
    the cardboard on each one of these lines. (See illustration) These slits will hold the yarn.

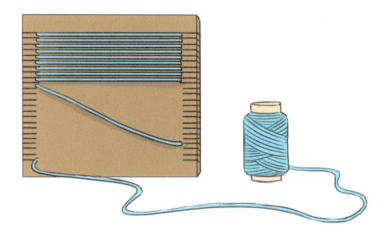

Begin with a large ball of yarn and anchor it in the first slit. Then wrap the yarn around the
    cardboard, anchoring in the slits each time. When finished, tie the beginning thread and the
    ending thread in a knot on the back of the weaving.

Spatial Art:

You will now take a different color of yarn and begin weaving. You can use a plastic needle or just go up and down with your fingers. You should go over one string and under the next, all the way across. Then when you start back the other way, you go over the one that was previously under and under the ones that were previously over. This makes a tight weave.

As you end a yarn and begin another, you can hide the threads by drawing your needle through the part that is already woven or you can tie small knots. When you have completed the weaving, you should tie all loose ends so that it doesn't unravel. You can then remove it from the cardboard loom.

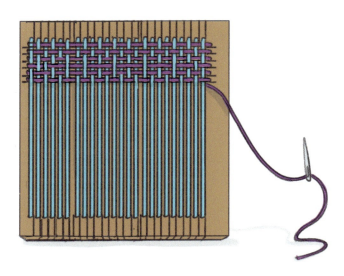

The Weaver by B. M. Franklin

My Life is but a weaving
Between my Lord and me.
I cannot choose the colors,
He weaves so steadily.

Sometimes a strand of sorrow
Is added to the plan,
And though it's difficult for us,
We still must understand
For He can view the pattern
Upon the upper side,
While we must look from underneath
And trust in Him to guide…

Not till the loom is silent
And the shuttles cease to fly
Will God roll back the canvas
And explain the reasons why

The dark threads are as needed
In the Weaver's skillful hand
As the threads of gold and silver
In the pattern He has planned.

In the poem, what do you think it means when the poem says, *The dark threads are as needed In the Weaver's skillful hand As the threads of gold and silver In the pattern He has planned.*

Interpersonal: Social

Be an angel for someone today…

Is there someone who needs help? If it is winter, does someone need their walk shoveled or does someone need help getting their mail? Does a younger sibling need help getting their boots on? If it is summer, is there someone who needs help with their gardens or picking up sticks in their yard. Maybe you could help your family with laundry or picking up trash or putting your toys away.

These are just a few suggestions. Think of other ways that you could be of service to someone.

Intrapersonal: Self

Simple meditation technique
Start simple.
Pick a time. Not an exact time of day, but a general time, like morning when
   you wake up, or at night before going to sleep.
Find a quiet spot.
Sit comfortably.
Start with just 1 or 2 minutes.
Take 3 breaths to begin. Just breath in and out slowly.
Let your mind rest. Allow your thoughts to be calm.
Take 3 breaths to end.

Meditation can help children read and respond to internal signals of stress before their developing brains and bodies give in to a full-blown tantrum. The key is intuiting what your child needs to come back into balance and giving him or her the tools to practice. Breathing is a calming mechanism.

In today's high-tech, fast-paced world, it's pretty easy to become over-stimulated. Busy schedules directing us to go, go, go and electronic devices constantly in our hands, pulling us into scattered digital directions make inner-peace a fleeting desire.

Musical way to end a meditation

Thanks a lot by Raffe

Thanks a lot
Thanks for the sun in the sky
Thanks a lot
Thanks for the birds
Thanks a lot
Thanks for the wind
Can continue with animals, land, people, moon, stars, and the way I feel.

Spiritual practice

It is important for all of us to have a spiritual practice or quieting routine.
Practices can include such things as prayer, connecting with nature, meditation, or attending a gathering of like-minded individuals.

It is so important to teach
children, as well as adults, to just be…
It is important to just breathe… The hope is that
you and your child will take a walk or take some time
to sit or lie down and just be with nature. How does it feel
to be outdoors in the fresh air and breathe in deeply? What
do you observe? Is there a breeze? Do you hear any nature
sounds? Do you see any clouds? Do you see any shapes in the
clouds? How do you feel about the shapes you see? How
do you feel about this experience? Has this experience
inspired a conversation with your child or with
another adult?

Closure:

The children should be encouraged to discuss their experiences with the book and the activities in these lessons. It is important to be accepting of all responses and to allow children to reflect and look at the world differently and to make connections with the natural world.

What did you learn about your child or your relationship during your conversations? As the parent or grandparent, what insight did you gain about your child or about yourself?

Reflect on all of the conversations and discussions. What insight have you gained about our interconnectedness with all things?

Epilogue

My hope is that you have enjoyed these activities and that they have inspired wonderful and meaningful conversations between you and your child. As you reflect on the time that you and your child spent preparing and engaging in the activities, I hope that you find new questions and deepening thought revolving around the overall theme of interconnectedness and seeing Love everywhere in everything.

In addition, I hope that the participants begin to notice their environment from a little different perspective and that they can continue to look at the world with wide-eyed wonder and enthusiasm. As a society, we have many things in common and we have challenges and varied experiences, but it is my hope that we can focus on our commonalities, our universal hopes and dreams, our love, and our peaceful places.

Dr. Miller explains this in her book, *The Spiritual Child.*

> *Bring the living world to your child by delighting in the relationships of nature. Live with animals, whether as indoor pets or familiar outdoor neighbors you come to know. Talk with animals. Actively engage in the sanctification of nature by openly celebrating it and its contribution to your family and the world we live in. Listening to trees, thinking that the wind has something to show you, knowing that the weather is not separate from who we are: part of the universal oneness is having respectful and loving relationships with nature and animals. Children can learn that all living things are our teachers; we can learn from their wisdom, judgment and sensibilities. (Lisa Miller, PhD. 341)*

As Joan Chittister, OSB, reminds us...

> *A true spirituality of creation, one that does not see creation as a single finished point in time, gives us the right to grow. It implies not only a God who made us, but a God who is with us, in us, and in everything around us. Whoever we are, whatever we are, this God knows us, understands us, walks with us to the melting point where what we are and what God is become one.*
> *(Joan Chittister, OSB, 196)*

May you share many wonderful conversations and experiences as you share and work together doing the activities in this book.

> *Give your children long peaceful moments to know firsthand a relationship with nature.*
> *(Lisa Miller, PhD. 341)*

May each of us find time to ponder our surroundings and our natural environment, to feel the breath of Spirit in our lives and to allow that peace to enfold us.

References

Chittister, J. D. (2004). *Called to Question: A Spiritual Memoir.* Sheed and Ward Publications, NY.

Einstein, A. (1879-1955). *On Living Life and Miracles.* Gurteen Community.

Gardner, H. (1983). *Frames of Mind: The Theory of Multiple Intelligences.* Basic Books, NY.

Kilmer, J. (1914 Ed.). *Trees and Other Poems.* Gutenburg eBook. NY.

Miller, L. (2015). *The Spiritual Child: The New Science of Parenting for Health and Lifelong Thriving.* St. Martin's Press, NY.

Author: Marian S. Taylor

Marian S. Taylor, EdD, is a retired university professor. Her career began at the elementary level where she taught first grade and served as a reading specialist. She was director of the university laboratory school and a chairperson of a university department. She taught undergraduate and graduate classes while at the university and spent many years directing the program for the development of reading specialists.

Marian has been very involved with her family and with church activities. She is the mother of three grown children and is very proud of her grandchildren. Other publications can be viewed at www.marianstaylorbooks.com.

Illustrator: Amy Duarte

Amy Duarte began her career as an artist working for Walt Disney Animation Studios. From there, she leapt into the world of visual effects and graphic arts on more than 35 feature films like *Pirates of the Caribbean: At World's End, The Amazing Spiderman, Mr. and Mrs. Smith*, etc. She was appointed as a lead artist for several major motion pictures, including *Fantastic Four*, where she advised and guided a team of artists on creating the special effects of Jessica Alba's character (Sue Storm).

Born in Jakarta, Indonesia, and raised in three different countries, Amy is fluent in six languages and an avid polo player. She is currently busy working on the next *Indiana Jones* movie. Her portfolio can be viewed at www.amyduarte.com.

Acknowledgments

I would like to acknowledge the beauty and everlasting oneness that I feel with the Divine. That interconnectedness sustains me and brings forth the concepts presented in these books. As the words tumbled onto the pages, I felt deep gratitude and love for the infinite grace offered. It is my hope that each experience with these materials will awaken awareness of the Divine in action and that the readers will begin to notice their surroundings and receive the infinite love offered.

I would like to express my sincere appreciation to Amy Duarte. She has been an amazing and imaginative illustrator for my children's book series which includes a set of seven children's books: *Coming Down, Looking Up, I Am With You All Ways, See Only Love, We Are the Trees, Messages in the Clouds, Angels Amongst Us*, and *Where There Is Love, We Are One*, this book of activities: *Your Heart is Calling, Raise a Heart-Centered Child: Activities to Inspire Family Conversations About our Interconnectedness*, and a set of cards: *Heart Call: Positive Action for Daily Living*, all of which are intended to inspire children's awareness. Amy has been wonderful to work with and has become a dear friend in the process. She was always flexible and creative as we worked through a variety of situations.

As I wrote the books and passages, I depended on my husband, Don, my children, Elizabeth, Jon, and Matthew, and my dear friend, Kathy Szymanowski. Their individual expertise in special needs, the law, and matters of the soul were invaluable. They would read and scrutinize the presentation of content and offer suggestions and reflections. These first reads were critical to the overall outcome of the series.
In addition, I am grateful to Colleen Holmes who spent many hours editing the books and bringing her expertise to the writing so that the finished product would be perfectly aligned.

As I began the creative elements of writing and composing the poetry that expressed the concepts, I gained inspiration from my children and grandchildren. Many of the illustrations are specifically in the likeness of my grandchildren and their parents as they expressed the words and actions that I portray in the books. All of the sign language illustrations, in *See Only Love*, were modeled by my oldest granddaughter, Evelyn Beckman. She provided so much insight into how children could gain awareness of their surroundings through the simple act of bringing concepts to their attention. I am blessed by our conversations and the thoughtful expressions from all of my amazing family.

Publications by Marian S. Taylor

Children's Literature Series
Coming Down, Looking Up
I AM With You All Ways
See Only Love
We Are the Trees
Messages in the Clouds
Angels Amongst Us
Where There Is Love, We Are One

Activity Book to Accompany Children's Literature Series
Your Heart is Calling: Raise a Heart-Centered Child: Activities to Inspire
Family Conversations About our Interconnectedness

Cards for Children
Heart Call: Positive Action for Daily Living

Devotional Guide
LIFTED: Into Christ's Arms for Mission and Service